GINGER PRIDE

A REDHEADED HISTORY OF THE WORLD

BY TOBIAS ANTHONY

Smith
Street
Books

CON-TENTS

INTRO-
DUC-
TION

You've heard of a redhead before, haven't you? You've heard of a 'ginger'? No doubt, you're familiar with some lesser PC invectives, too: 'carrot-top', 'Fanta pants', 'ginger pubes', 'red knob', 'fire-crotch', 'Ronald' (as in McDonald), 'red', and even 'simply red'. And then, of course, there is the ultimate nickname/insult one-two punch: 'ranga'. Most people will either tell you that ranga derives from the word 'orange' or that it comes from 'orangutan', and depending on the chosen derivation the phrase is considered either mildly harmless or the greatest of grievous insults.

But why so many names for a group of people with an unusual, yet natural, tint to their hair? And why has so much energy been expended thinking up insults for them?

Well, the mythos of redheadedness runs more than follicle deep. In fact, it plays a hand in almost every aspect of the world as we know it – from the Vikings, to the occult, to witch trials, to the royal family, to modern medicine. Even Hitler took the time to weigh in, supposedly banning the union between redheads. And *South Park* creators Matt Stone and Trey Parker have had plenty to say about gingers, specifically regarding on what day we should *kick* them.

Are redheads really all that bad? What exactly is their deal?

If you believe the rumours, gingers are hot-tempered and prone to anger – little sacks of violence just waiting to unleash their Berserker rage. This theory about the hot-blooded nature of redheads has existed for centuries. We didn't include it in the list of nicknames above because it's an antiquated term, but in Australia 'blue' and/or 'bluey' were also common names for redheads. Bluey was less a slur and more an affectionate nickname, but its origins were nonetheless entangled with the pervasive idea that gingers, particularly Irishmen, were a fighting lot. The term 'blue', in fact, was a substitute word for 'fight' during the era.

Regardless of the accuracy of these conceptions, the fact is that the world is host to a large number of redheads – 140 million, in fact – and society has simply got to learn to cohabit with the blighters. Statistically speaking, redheads are thought to make up a mere 2 per cent of the world's population, with 18 million residing in the United States alone. But proportionately speaking, it's the Celtic nations that lead the way – roughly 10 per cent of the population of Scotland, Ireland and Wales is made up of gingers.

Of course, there has been no official census taken, but small groupings of studies show that red hair is also relatively common in northern European nations, such as England, Iceland and Norway, while northern France, Sweden, Germany, The Netherlands and Finland all rank ahead of global averages in the percentage of their population boasting gingers. And don't rule out Russia, either. The Volga region hosts more gingers per capita than anywhere else in the world, except Ireland. And red hair is also common among Ashkenazi Jews.

Still, it's hard to get away from that global figure: 2 per cent. It doesn't seem like a lot, does it? And yet there exists an entire culture surrounding the carrot-top. In fact, gingers are seemingly *over*-represented within society, inhabiting numerous public roles, including film stars, famous authors, politicians and comedians. This might suggest that redheads have a preternatural instinct for success. Or perhaps society favours the redhead after all ...

Ginger Pride brings together everything you've ever wanted or needed to know about redheads, detailing their past, present and, hopefully, very bright future. There's something extra appealing

IN FACT, GINGERS ARE SEEMINGLY OVER-REPRESENTED WITHIN SOCIETY, INHABITING NUMEROUS PUBLIC ROLES, INCLUDING FILM STARS, FAMOUS AUTHORS, POLITICIANS AND COMEDIANS.

about the colour red – it signifies intensity, heat, passion, even sexuality – and there's no more exotic human out there than the ginger of now. So, strap yourself in and get reading. By the end of this book you might just be raising a fist of solidarity as you cry:

IT'S GAELIC FOR:

REDHEADS FOREVER!

1.
THE WAY OF THE GINGER

First things first. Before we begin our journey to get to the heart of all matters ginger, we think it's only right to come to terms with the modern redhead – who they are, where you're likely to find them and, of course, all the dos and don'ts when engaging with one.

IDENTIFICATION GUIDE

MIRROR, MIRROR ON THE WALL,
WHO IS THE REDDEST OF THEM ALL?

1. STRAWBERRY-BLONDE

2. AUBURN

3. COPPER

4. MAROON

5. APRICOT

6. CRIMSON

7. SUN-KISSED

8. BURGUNDY

9. CHERRY

10. FIRE-ENGINE

11. SUNBURST

12. SUNSET

13. MAHOGANY

14. GINGER

15. ROSE GOLD

16. RED VELVET

17. RUBY

18. POISON APPLE

19. AUBERGINE
(AKA: SUPER FAKE)

20. CLASSIC

1.   2.   3.   4.   5.

6.   7.   8.   9.   10.

11.   12.   13.   14.   15.

16.   17.   18.   19.   20.

11

A SPOTTER'S GUIDE

Gingers come in many incarnations. Here's a quick overview of some that you may encounter.

THE NATURE CHILD

If the nose and naval piercings weren't enough, the bare feet and nest-like mound of ginger dreadlocks atop her head complete the picture. She's been dancing in circles at a psy-trance festival in the forest for the past five days, but even though she smells a little off-colour, she's everybody's favourite reefer-smoking university dropout.

THE 21ST CENTURY VIKING

The days of raping and pillaging are behind us, thank God, but this guy's still intimidating. He's a mammoth-man built for war, but now that he's grown out that luscious hipster beard and donned its requisite accompaniment, the flannel shirt, he's kind of cuddly-looking, too.

FRECKLES

You've seen this little girl before, smiling sweetly at you from some family-centric commercial promoting cleaning products or Mum's home-cooking. *Oh, what a delight to behold! She's Grandfather's favourite grandchild.*

THE SNOT-NOSED BRAT

This little boy has a grubby face and a runny nose, and for some unknown reason his knees are always covered in mud ... What's he got himself into this time? And what's he doing now? He's a very naughty young man!

THE NERD

He's lean, but not very mean, and right now he's distracted, furiously pressing the buttons on his computer. It's clear that he's never run a comb through his hair – not once! Treat this one with kid-gloves. He's delicate. And he might very well be some kind of genius.

THE ACADEMIC

This wine-quaffing sophisticate might seem alluring – her hair falls either side of her face in a neat bob, framing those chic cat-eye glasses – but be warned: she's actually very, *very* boring. Stay clear!

THE SILVER FOX

This stately gent doesn't have golden, orangey locks anymore, but he once did. You can tell from his light salt-and-pepper hair, his freckled skin and his coquettish face. And because he looks exactly like Robert Redford. (Okay, so it's Robert Redford.) But the aged ginger poses an intriguing question: when the greying commences, does one cease to be a redhead?

THE FRAUD

It's dyed! It's dyed! It's dyed!, we tell you. Get out of here, tryhard!

THE 21ST CENTURY ROYAL

In a past life she would've been a queen, or at the very least, an excellent princess, but there aren't many royal positions available these days. She'll have to settle for being the embodiment of celebrity glamour, instead. Sharp, angular and super-stylish, she's an all-knowing and all-powerful *femme de force* (that's French for amazing lady, right?). Just don't go writing this one off as some mere 'bombshell', though – she's got the brains to boot.

THE TRAITOR

He's dyed his ginger mop black to fit in with his emo friends, but there's no hiding that pasty skin, or those freckles across the bridge of his nose and on his knuckles. He's a traitor to the cause!

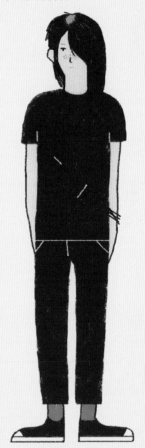

REDHEADS IN THE WILD:

WHERE ARE YOU MOST LIKELY TO SPOT A GINGER?

Given that their vampiric tendencies keep them clinging to the shadows (well, technically it's their fair skin, but whatever), there are more places you're not likely to spot a redhead than places you will.

So, where are they not? Well, they're not at your local tanning salon, that's for sure. Nor are they rocking out at Burning Man or chilling at the beach. In fact, they're rarely seen outdoors in any capacity. (Okay, maybe this is a slight exaggeration, but we're doing our best to help you locate them, and with only 2 per cent of the global population being ginger, you're going to need to narrow your search.)

Here are the three places you're most likely to discover the 21st century ginger at work, rest and/or play.

PARTY TIME: THE PUB

Gingers party, too. In fact, they party hard! When the world is stacked against you, you've gotta get loose sometimes, and a ginger has gotta get *turnt*, gotta get *lit*, just like anybody else.

You're likely to find at least one or two gingers at any public house or bar, especially a dimly-lit, Celtic-themed one. You know the type – mahogany bar, whisky bottles lined up behind it, and the walls are still yellow from the cigarette smoke of yesteryear. It's a place that smells like Old Pulteney and sounds like old men, who are invariably in there too, browsing the racing form at the back of the newspaper (yeah, they still read those).

EXERCISE: ROLLER-SKATING RINK, INDOOR ROCK-CLIMBING WALL, GYM

Gingers need exercise, too. And they also need an avenue for heroic displays of physical prowess. Redheads tend to prefer the calm and sun-proof environs of an indoor sports facility. Besides, why exercise outdoors when you can reap the same benefits somewhere you're not prey to turns in weather, and where a multitude of refreshments are available at the kiosk?

Gingers are a little bit ahead of the curve when it comes to amenities and weather conditions, having grown up hyper-aware of the sun, ever-vigilant about the application of sunscreen.

It's likely that gingers will lead the way, with all sports in the future being held and played indoors. Let's face it, inside is just, like, way better than outside.

CHILL SPOTS: LIVING ROOM, MAN-CAVE, *REAL* CAVE

Whether it's a night in on the couch getting their Netflix-and-chill on or tinkering about restoring an old car, gingers are staying indoors – *always*! So, if you plan on finding some redheads in the wild but don't feel up to committing a home invasion, there's one last resort: finding some actual, *real* caves.

It's long been thought that communities of redheads not yet discovered by civilisation are living somewhere out there, in the wild, and it stands to reason that they're probably holed up in a cave somewhere. So, if you're keen to put your ginger-spotting efforts to good use, don't forget to pack your gear and get ready to go spelunking!

HOW TO AUTHENTICATE YOUR GINGER:
IDENTIFYING A FAKE OR A TRAITOR

Perhaps the most important aspect of ginger identification is being able to spot a natural redhead, while also being able to identify those redheads who have opted out of gingerdom by dyeing their hair another colour entirely.

As you'll discover in the upcoming segment on etiquette, there are some things you just can't say or do around a redhead. Asking, *So, are you a natural ginger?* is one of them. Sure, it might make life simpler overall, but think of this question from a different perspective. After all, you wouldn't stop a brunette in the street and ask them if they were a natural brunette, now would you?

THE FAKE

Spotting the difference between a natural redhead and a fake is no easy feat. Take the actresses Isla Fisher and Amy Adams, for example. Do you think both are naturally red? Here's the truth: Amy Adams is actually a fake, while Isla Fisher is a natural born, 100 per cent authentic ginger.

There are dead giveaways, of course, such as colours that don't occur in nature – any hair colour that tends towards shades of purple or violet is an obvious sign of follicle fakery. But on the whole, modern hairdressers are pretty darn good at blending non-natural gingers into the redheaded community. Perhaps the bigger question at play here is ... why?

Given that redheads are much maligned, why would anybody want to join them? Especially when natural-born gingers are prone to enact their own brand of elitism against such interlopers. *They don't really know what life as a ginger is! They haven't gone through the years of torment!* There's even a nickname given to fake redheads: 'daywalkers'. This, of course, is a play on the alleged vampiric tendencies of natural gingers. It's not clear who first coined the term, given that it's vaguely insulting to both parties of red.

While it's true that the fake ginger may not be carrying the emotional baggage from years of teasing or any other such baptism of fire, a person who chooses to dye their hair red is someone who sees the positive qualities of gingerdom. This is something that should be championed – not only is this person paying a compliment to the redheaded community, they are acting as a beacon of approval for the much-maligned hair colour. And given that their numbers are thought to be dwindling, shouldn't the two-per-centers be encouraging anyone to jump on board?

Perhaps the main thing to watch out for – the real giveaway that a redhead is a fake – is an elevated level of self-confidence. From a young age, the natural ginger is conditioned to believe that they embody all the redhead clichés, but rarely are they taught anything about self-worth. By this measure, anyone with red hair who hasn't been conditioned to live out such clichés, and especially anyone who isn't dragging around a whole mess of emotional baggage, can't possibly be a natural. Come on, it's basic common sense ...

THE TRAITOR

This one is certainly easier to detect than the fake. It's amazing how strongly disparaging the redheaded community is of anyone who dyes their hair in order to leave their gingerness behind. These people are often the most ostracised. They are considered traitors to the cause, sell-outs, abominations!

The signs are obvious, and were outlined in our spotter's guide (page 12), but to quickly recap, one is looking for a drastic and/or suspicious contrast between pasty skin tone and hair colour.

Other features to look out for include light eyebrows, as well as clusters of freckles on the bridge of the nose or across the knuckles. You don't have to be Sherlock to detect this one, trust us.

But what's so bad about this really? Well, for natural redheads who have lived through the hazing and ignored strong suggestions that they should dye their hair, and have matured into adulthood proud of their freak follicles, shying away from such a genetic predisposition is perceived as a weakness and a betrayal. It's not easy being red, but it's certainly a lot harder with a turncoat in the mix, and here the mob mentality reigns supreme: all gingers must suffer in equal measure.

There is an undeniable bravery to being ginger and proud, especially when you hear stories of sexual rejection, and of parents so disparaging of their children's hair colour that they have tried to bleach it out (yes, this has actually happened!). So it's no wonder the ginger community can't accept a traitor. It's all about backbone, dammit!

MATTERS OF ETIQUETTE

There are some things you just don't say or do.
We all know that. And specifically, there are some things
you should never say or do in front of a ginger. You know,
unless you want to provoke their ire.

DON'T DO THIS	DO THIS INSTEAD
Don't mention the redheaded stepchild. This one's fairly straightforward, but for those not in the know, the phrase 'redheaded stepchild' has long been used as shorthand for 'unwanted child'. The idea is that a person's redheadedness stands them apart from a majority (whether the microcosm of a family, or society more broadly), implying that redheadedness also makes a person unlikeable, maybe even unloveable.	**Instead: Say something inclusive.** If you are compelled to note someone's otherness by way of their ginger locks, why not try saying something positive? As the old saying goes: if you don't have anything good to say, don't say anything at all. That rule applies here, too.

Don't ask: 'Does the carpet match the drapes?' It's just plain icky. Asking anyone about the colour of their pubic hair is an absolute no-no. You wouldn't ask anybody else, so don't ask a ginger.	**Instead: Say nothing.** There's no replacement for this one. In fact, complimenting someone's pubic hair might be even worse … and creepy! Super creepy!
Don't confide: 'I've never slept with a redhead before.' Ah, yes, people love being bucket-list items, don't they? No? Really?	**Instead: Use another pick-up line.** If what you're driving at is that you find someone attractive, maybe just say so.
Don't ask: 'Is it true that redheads have fiery tempers?' This classic cliché is likely to elicit either a wince or a punch.	**Instead: Think! For once in your life, just think.** If you believe the answer to this question might be a 'yes', then what do you think asking this question might do?
Don't say: 'I'm not into redheads' OR 'I don't find redheads attractive.' Little explanation is needed here, but you might be surprised just how often this is uttered. It makes people feel bad and insecure, so maybe just don't say it.	**Instead: Keep it to yourself.** Consider how this would sound if you swapped 'redhead' for an ethnic group. Mmm, yep …
Don't say: 'I've heard redheads are really wild in the sack.' Okay, so we live in a world that's pretty hung up about sex, but dammit, what is with the redheaded community and such cultural sexualisation?	**Instead: Say something normal.** SERIOUSLY. JUST. SAY. SOMETHING. NORMAL!!!!!!!

Don't draw this comparison: 'Has anyone ever told you that you look like X?' Here, 'X' stands in place of any redheaded person ever (popular comparisons tend to include Mick Hucknall and Prince Harry for males, and almost any popular current actress for women). This ginger faux pas should probably have been at the top of this list.	**Instead: Comparison is the thief of joy, so like most items on this list, we would generally suggest that you keep your mouth shut.** Given that such comparisons are an everyday occurrence in the life of a ginger, if you really want to impress them, try making a comparison between them and someone who doesn't have red hair. You know, someone that person might actually look like …
Don't draw the attention of your redheaded friend to the presence of another redhead nearby. Why do this? What's the point? Why do you assume one ginger cares about the location of another? (Well, they do, but …)	**Instead: Don't do anything.** This is a particularly odd one, but it's a constant to the ginger experience. *Oh, look, she has hair like you do!* Huh?
Don't reference anything concerning the occult, witches, Satan or that rumour that redheads don't have souls.	**A hug might be nice. Otherwise, asking after a redhead's wellbeing will suffice.**
Don't ask: 'Do you want redheaded babies?' The implication here kind of connects to the faux pas listed above – the idea that redheadedness is unwanted, perhaps even burdensome.	**Instead: Make it a positive!** Try saying this instead: *I hope you have redheaded babies. That would be so cute!*

Don't ask: 'Are you going to find a redheaded partner?'
Right, because redheads should only ever intermingle. We don't want the bloodlines getting crossed or anything ...

Instead: Pick another topic.
As strange as it might seem, this question is commonly put to gingers, as is this one: *Do you find redheads attractive?* It's hard to decipher the intended meaning here, but you can rest assured it's fairly offensive, given that these questions serve to accentuate the 'novelty' of redheadedness. Regardless of how curious you might be, it's best to leave this line of interrogation alone.

Don't use any of the following words, phrases or nicknames:
Fire-crotch, Fanta pants, Ranga, Red knob, Carrot-top, Freckles, Ginger or Red.

Instead: Just don't.
Call people by their real names. People have names, you know.

If anything remains unclear then we prescribe the following: Listen to Tim Minchin's song 'Taboo'. It will clarify all ginger etiquette in four pleasurable minutes. We honestly can't recommend it strongly enough.

FAMOUS OR ROYALTY?

When it comes to identifying the ginger, one can't look past their connections to both royalty and celebrity. And given that in today's landscape of reality television and pop culture iconography, celebrity and royalty are essentially one and the same, we thought we'd break down some of those connections. Perhaps your ginger friend is set for stardom ...

ORIGINS:

REDHEADS AND ROYALTY ...

So many of the Tudors had, or at least have been portrayed as having, red hair. Descriptions from the day, as well as artistic renderings, suggest a link between royalty and gingerness. Plus, the medieval standard for beauty was a golden-red hair colouring throughout the time period.

ROYAL REDS ...

The list of redheaded royals is mighty long, but here are a few: Elizabeth Woodville, Elizabeth of York, Henry VIII, Henry VIII's brother Arthur, Mary I, James V, Lady Jane Grey, Lettice Knollys, Prince Harry.

SO, DOES HAVING RED HAIR MAKE YOU A ROYAL?

In some cases, it might! Well, sort of. What is incredible to note is that by the time Queen Elizabeth I passed away, England had seen 139 consecutive years of redheaded royal reign, with either a ginger king or queen in power for well over a century.

THE IMPACT OF ROYAL REDS ...

Given that gingers were so synonymous with the monarchy, it seems likely that this established some social conditioning. Men and women of the time would probably have found redheadedness to be a sign of high status, helping gingers to thrive and the gene to live on. This same form of social conditioning might just be seen in today's celebrity culture ...

IS IT EASIER TO BECOME FAMOUS AS A REDHEAD?

Given the proclivity for famous non-gingers to go red, we think there must be something about being a redhead that enhances fame and appeal. It seems that, for those at the top, being redheaded is a great advantage, and it's this tradition of redheads in the spotlight that has helped shape and build the clichéd characteristics we now recognise and love.

FAMOUS BOTTLED REDS

The likes of Rita Hayworth, Molly Ringwald, Christina Hendricks, Lucille Ball and Amy Adams have all adopted their rufosity in order to benefit themselves professionally, and in doing so have boosted the profile of redheads the world over.

EFFECTS OF THE 'BOTTLE-TOP'...

The adoption of gingerness by celebrity icons has helped promote certain stereotypes that natural redheads benefit from today, giving them, in the words of author and ginger expert Jacky Colliss Harvey, *'permission to be confident, kooky, screwball, impulsive, hot-blooded and passionate'.*

THE GROWING POPULARITY OF BOTTLED RED ...

The numbers speak for themselves. In the United States alone, red hair dye sells more than any other colour on the market, and generates $200 million in sales per year.

WHY RED?

The colour red is thought to set off a reward-seeking instinct in humans, which is why it's often used by advertisers in commercials. Perhaps this goes some way towards explaining why so many gingers often find themselves at the top despite comprising such a slim percentage of the global population.

HAIR VS FAME

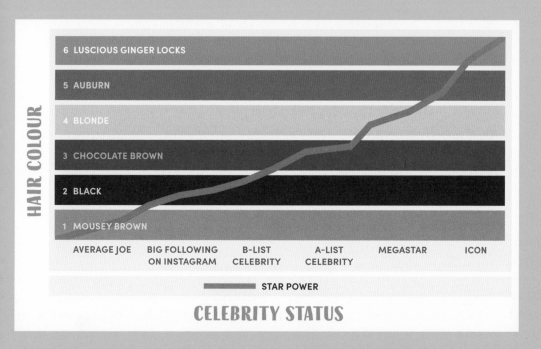

HAIR COLOUR

6	LUSCIOUS GINGER LOCKS
5	AUBURN
4	BLONDE
3	CHOCOLATE BROWN
2	BLACK
1	MOUSEY BROWN

AVERAGE JOE   BIG FOLLOWING ON INSTAGRAM   B-LIST CELEBRITY   A-LIST CELEBRITY   MEGASTAR   ICON

—— STAR POWER

CELEBRITY STATUS

ALL YE GINGERS REJOICE!

GINGERISM OR GINGERPHOBIA?

If you haven't heard either of these terms before, it's time to get familiar with them. And if you're wondering if this is a joke, the answer is no. This is real life. How seriously people regard these terms depends on who you're dealing with, but be warned: in the ginger community, some people take this stuff very seriously. Political correctness gone mad? Maybe. A reality of the times? Most definitely.

GINGERISM

Gingerism refers to the discrimination against and/or prejudice towards people 'of' red hair. It's kind of like racism, only for gingers.

Signs that you're a gingerist may include:

- generalising that all redheads are creepy or disgusting
- assuming a male redhead is a geeky virgin, and thus less manly
- thinking it's okay to ask redheads intimate questions, such as asking about their pubic hair
- assuming they're in on the joke and *should* adopt your prescribed nickname.

GINGERPHOBIA

Gingerphobia is the fear of redheaded people. It commonly manifests as social rejection, and is thought to be an underlying symptom of gingerism. A study in Ireland has shown that a staggering 60.6 per cent of males and 47.3 per cent of females have experienced discrimination on account of their ginger follicles.

Signs that you're gingerphobic might include:

- finding redheads unattractive and thus being repulsed by the idea of their proximity
- lashing out at redheads in the street, hurling abuse like a paranoid member of an angry mob
- having a complete and total mistrust of the redheaded community
- inventing, propagating or believing ginger conspiracies.

In recent times, the ginger community has begun actively combating gingerism and gingerphobia. The emergence of the Red Hot British Boy calendar, featuring a plethora of Britain's best-looking ginger males, is helping redheads take a proactive stance against their malignment. There have also been photography exhibitions in France and the UK dedicated to spreading a positive ginger message. Most recently, there has even been a petition set up through change.org advocating for the creation of a redheaded emoji.

So, is gingerism a real thing? Let's just say that people don't go to these kinds of lengths to shape and rebrand their image for nothing.

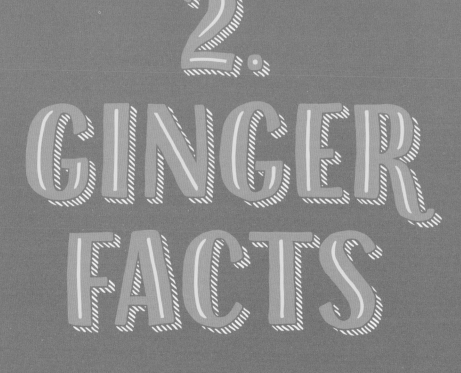

2.
GINGER
FACTS

The world of red is more immersive than a first glance would suggest. Outside of the cultural understanding many of us possess about redheads – the stereotypes regarding their temper, the myths concerning their genetic predispositions – there is a plethora of ginger-specific dates, activities and events to get familiar with. Yes, they have their own online dating services. Yes, apps have been made in their honour. And, yes, there are days of the year dedicated to both kicking them and kissing them.

GINGERPHOBIA, GINGERISM AND GINGER FETISHISTS

Listed here are five everyday, ginger-related thingums for you to familiarise yourself with. You will also discover several key dates on the ginger calendar, accompanied by a breakdown of a handful of the most important ones.

EVERYDAY, GINGER-RELATED THINGUMS ...

GINGERTUBE

HOTFORGINGER.COM

Are you a ginger, or a ginger aficionado? Are you looking for love? Well, hotforginger.com is the site for you – a ginger-finding dating database for gingers and ginger-lovers alike.

The website was founded in 2010 by Marc Crouch, a Londoner and fellow redhead, who thought the ginger population needed a community all of its own, as well as a community invested in promoting a positive message about the world of gingerdom.

hotforginger.com isn't just a dating site, though. Comprising blogs, commentary and endorsements related to all things red, it's a lifestyle epicentre dedicated to flying the ginger flag.

GINGER BOOTH IPHONE APP

Not a natural redhead? Ever wondered what you'd look like as one? Well, with the Ginger Booth iPhone app, redheadedness is only a tap and a swipe away ...

First, you take a selfie on your phone. Moments later, with a little digital trickery, your face is transformed into that of a ginger – pasty skin, freckles and all. We don't know whether to protest the novelty of this one or to take pride in the innocent homage.

GINGERPARROT.CO.UK

Ginger Parrot is an online super-community dedicated to all things red. Established in 2009, Ginger Parrot has become one of the go-to places for redheads and redhead lovers seeking the latest in ginger-specific news, photography, info and feature articles. The website also boasts an online store, and is available across multiple social media platforms, including Facebook, Instagram, Pinterest and Twitter, all dedicated to spreading the good word on – as they put it – *all things nice and gingerful.*

REDHEADS ANONYMOUS

Redheads Anonymous is an award-winning comedic web series about identity, stereotypes and what it means to be ginger. The series follows protagonist Molly as she vies to win a redhead scholarship, exploring, with the help of her three ginger pals, all facets of the world of gingerdom along the way.

This comedy web series is certainly worth a look. The episodes can be found online at redheadsanonymous.com. (Additionally, you can find Redheads Anonymous on Twitter, Tumblr and YouTube.)

*~~GINGER PORN~~ ... ADULT GINGER-THEMED ENTERTAINMENT

Perhaps the less said about this one the better. But it's a thing. Trust us. It's a thing ...

KEY DATES ON THE GINGER CALENDAR

KICK A GINGER DAY

Arguably the best-known ginger-themed calendar date, Kick a Ginger Day was inspired by the animated comedy series *South Park*. The episode in question, titled 'Ginger Kids', saw series antagonist Eric Cartman fuelling hatred towards gingers everywhere. So much so, in fact, that some school-aged fans of the show went on to assault their ginger peers in the real world, drawing international outrage and condemnation.

Thankfully, things have cooled down since the episode first aired, and most people are able to see the lighter side of this event. There's even a dedicated website – kick-a-ginger-day.com – which, in the spirit of good-natured pot-stirring, warns against taking the day seriously. An orange banner at the top of the page says: *Kick-a-ginger-day is not a serious event. It's a joke which originated from South Park. Don't kick anyone, we love gingers!* The website also sells various merchandise, from mugs to T-shirts, all of which display pro-ginger slogans such as *I ♥ gingers, Gingers do have souls!* and even *Jesus was a ginger.* How nice.

GINGERS DO HAVE SOULS

REDHEAD DAY FESTIVAL

This two-day summer festival takes place during the first weekend of September in Breda, a city in the Netherlands. The festival was established in 2005 by Dutch painter Bart Rouwenhorst, who created the event by accident while planning an upcoming exhibition. Mr Rouwenhorst, inspired by fellow artists such as Gustav Klimt and Dante Gabriel Rossetti, both of whom created famous paintings depicting redheaded women, was intending to exhibit his own series of paintings centred around redheads. But Bart had a problem – he needed models.

He placed an advertisement in a local newspaper looking for models with naturally red hair. He never expected to receive 150 responses ...

Mr Rouwenhorst's solution was to select 14 of the models, then take a group photo of the 150-strong who turned up and create a lottery that would select a fifteenth model by chance. Bart had so much fun that he decided to do the same again the following year and in so doing, he created the Redhead Day Festival. The event has since aimed to even up the sexes (given that the first included only women). Today, Redhead Day doesn't only celebrate red hair, but also focuses on art related to the colour red. The festivities include workshops, lectures and demonstrations, and entry is currently free of charge thanks to local government sponsorship. The festival includes participants from 50 countries across the globe, but to participate you must, of course, be a natural redhead.

INTERNATIONAL KISS A GINGER DAY

Is the date of 12 January important to you? No? Well, it should be, because 12 January is International Kiss a Ginger Day.

Kiss a Ginger Day was first started in 2009. It was developed by Derek Forgie as a Facebook group intended to offset the vitriol of the first Kick a Ginger Day, which had taken place in November the previous year. In Forgie's own words, Kiss a Ginger Day was thought up as a 'karmic counter-event'. It's a day intended to counter the negative attention often received by gingers, asking that we show nothing but love to our ginger-haired friends, family members or colleagues in an effort to bring a smile to their faces and make the world just that little bit nicer.

How to celebrate? Easy! First, mark your calendar. Second, find a redhead and plant one on them to show your appreciation of their genetic perfection. Just, you know, be sure to get their permission first ...

THE IRISH REDHEAD CONVENTION

The Irish Redhead Convention is held annually in County Cork, Ireland, during August. It was first created by redhead brother and sister Joleen and Denis Cronin in 2010. Held over three days, the event includes all manner of festivities and celebrations, including prizes for best (and reddest) eyebrows and for the most freckles, carrot-throwing competitions and orchestral concerts. Additionally, each year The Irish Redhead Convention crowns a ginger king and queen from participants and attendees.

Launched with the aim of bringing the redheaded community together, the convention boasts wide-reaching and global appeal. The celebration has attracted people from several continents and has become one of the best-known redhead festivals in the world, attracting media attention worldwide. The Irish Redhead Convention also raises awareness for both the Irish Cancer Society and the SunSmart campaign, while also promoting the region in which the festival is held, encouraging community pride and boosting economic activity.

Currently, however, due to the costs of running the event, as well as the demanding commitment required of volunteers, this festival is on hold while programmers seek ways to fund the event and manage its increased size and popularity. For more information, visit redheadconvention.com.

INTERNATIONAL GINGER PRIDE MARCHES AND OTHER IMPORTANT DATES

The ginger calendar is chock full of exciting events. Across the globe, several nations have incorporated pride marches into their annual calendars. See the list below for a ginger day near you.

WHAT?	WHERE?	WHEN?
Ginger Pride Belfast	Belfast, Northern Ireland	11 February
Ginger Pride Parade	Rome, Georgia, USA	18 March
Ginger Pride Rally	Melbourne, Australia	29 April
Redhead Event	Portland, USA	TBC
Redhead Day Germany	Hamburg, Germany	27 May
RossItalia	Milan, Italy	28–29 May
Redhead Days Chicago	Chicago, USA	10–11 June
Gingers: The Gathering	Plymouth, UK	August (exact date not yet available)
Dunbar WV Redhead Festival	Dunbar, West Virginia, USA	September (exact date not yet available)
National Meeting of Natural Redheads	Florianopolis, Brazil	9 September
Redhead Day UK	London, UK	next event: May 2018
League of Extraordinary Redheads	Troy, New York, USA	TBC

SCIENCE OR MYTH?

Think gingers can produce their own Vitamin D? Want to know the odds that you and your other half might produce one? Ever wondered if redheads have certain genetic predispositions, such as a higher risk of developing Parkinson's disease?

The answers await you ...

ARE REDHEADS REALLY DYING OUT?

Ah, the big one first. Much has been made of the prevalent rumour that the ginger community is 'dying out'. Popular pseudo-science states that global warming is contributing to the regression of the redhead gene – the mutated MC1R – especially given that redheads don't adapt well to warm climes.

In theory, there is a possibility that this is occurring, but there's no substantive data to support this. However, some tentative predictions state that the redhead gene could be extinct by as early as 2060.

While it's easy to blame global warming for this, it doesn't seem such a likely cause. It is more likely to be the reality of redheads living in a globalised, multicultural society, where their rare gene has a limited chance to thrive. But not necessarily. After all, the existence of redheads is said to be something that haunted Charles Darwin in his lifetime, because he wasn't able to fit gingers into his Survival of the Fittest theorem. And yet they are still around ...

WHAT IS THE SCIENCE BEHIND THEIR FIERINESS? AND WHY ARE THEY SO ANGRY?

There's no scientific evidence to support the notion that redheads have more fiery tempers than non-gingers. But if indeed it can be observed that they do, we can probably attribute this phenomenon to cultural and social conditioning.

The Ancient Greeks saw red hair as exemplifying courage and honour, and throughout history famous warriors and powerful figures have been characterised as gingers. For example, Homer's *Iliad* describes both the hero Achilles and Helen of Troy, the daughter of Zeus, as redheads. The Norse god Thor is also often described as a ginger. Culturally, such characterisations have evolved into myths about the temperament of all redheads, in many cases making them symbols of aggression and violence.

Scientifically speaking, redheads are thought to be better able to generate adrenaline. Apparently their cells can access adrenaline faster than people with other hair colours, which plays into the notion that they are fast to react. This would naturally be advantageous to those engaged in combat, which may have contributed to their warrior origins.

IS RED HAIR A RECESSIVE OR DOMINANT GENE? AND AM I A CARRIER?

The MC1R gene – the gene for red hair – is a recessive one. This means that a person needs two copies of the gene in order for it to be expressed.

Whether you're a carrier depends on who you are and your family's history. However, it is possible for families who have not seen a redhead in decades to suddenly find one in their midst, almost at random.

In the United States, for instance, it is believed that roughly 25 per cent of Caucasians carry the ginger gene, while in Ireland 40 per cent of the population are thought to carry it.

It is understood that families can carry a variant of the gene for generations, but it isn't until one carrier has children with another carrier that a carrot-top can materialise. In the UK, where redheads make up a higher proportion of the population than anywhere else in the world, the prevalence of the gene is likely to be high, also.

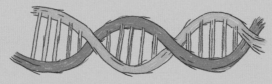

WILL MY BABY HAVE RED HAIR?

Well, that all depends on your genes, now doesn't it? As mentioned previously, it's not outside the realms of possibility for a family that hasn't seen a redhead for years to find themselves with a newborn ginger, just so long as the parents are carriers of the MC1R gene.

Here's how it breaks down:

- If you have red hair and have a child with someone who also has red hair, odds are that the child will have red hair, too. This is because both parents possess the recessive gene, which is being expressed by both parties.

- If one parent is a natural ginger and the other is not, but is also a carrier of MC1R, the chances of the child being born with red hair are about 50/50.

- If neither parent is red, but both carry the gene, then there's a one in four chance that the child will be born a carrot-top.

- And, finally, if one parent *does not* possess the MC1R gene, then there is simply no chance that their child will be born with red hair.

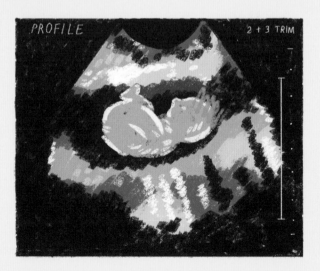

DON'T REDHEADS TECHNICALLY
HAVE LESS HAIR OVERALL?

Technically, yes. This is a bit of an odd one, but red hair is actually thicker than other colours. This means that on average redheads possess only 90,000 strands of follicular wonder, while blondes carry an average of 110,000 strands of hair and brunettes have roughly 140,000 strands. It's the thickness of red hair that compensates for their fewer strands, and which helps propagate the image of thick, luscious ginger locks that has become associated with the most attractive of rufous hairdos.

Bonus fact: *Not only is red hair thicker, it's also much more difficult to dye another colour. This is because red hair holds its natural pigment more strongly than other hues.*

DO REDHEADS SMELL DIFFERENT?

Yes. They smell *better*!

Redheads are said to have their own particular scent – another genetic factor that's based upon their more acid skin-mantle. Their scent is thought to be naturally sweeter and musk-like, but this scent is believed to change depending on their emotional state, too. Being so sweet, their scent is also thought to have aphrodisiac effects upon others, which is perhaps how gingers have come to be associated with lustfulness and virility.

Bonus fact: *Redheads are also said to exude more pleasant pheromones. Combine this with their natural aroma and it's easy to conclude that redheads are ... well, designed for certain things ...*

ARE REDHEADS MORE OR LESS SUSCEPTIBLE TO PAIN?

Redheads have demonstrated that they have different levels of sensitivity to pain compared with people who possess other hair colours. Operating-room doctors have noted that redheads require more anaesthetic to keep them from waking up during medical procedures – a whopping 20 per cent more than other people.

However, while they are commonly less sensitive to anaesthetics, particularly lidocaine injections, gingers are more sensitive to opiates, meaning that they actually need less of these types of painkillers for them to be effective.

In fact, redheads have greater sensitivity to a range of stimulus overall, including thermal pain, which is said to be caused by their naturally occurring low levels of Vitamin K. One study that measured the pain tolerance levels of redheads used heat-related pain as its litmus for overall sensitivity. The test found that gingers tend to feel things more acutely and more unpleasantly overall, which is thought to be the result of the MC1R gene. The mutation of this gene that results in redheadedness also releases a hormone that stimulates the brain receptor in charge of pain regulation.

Additionally, gingers generally have more sensitive teeth, and it's also believed that redheads bruise more easily than people of other hair colours. Large numbers of redheaded women, in particular, have reported this.

IS IT TRUE THAT REDHEADS CAN CHANGE THEIR BODY TEMPERATURE FASTER THAN OTHER PEOPLE?

As a side-effect of their increased sensitivity to thermal pain, gingers are better able to change their body temperature. It's said that redheads feel cold weather conditions more acutely than other people, so it makes sense that they may have developed a biological way to combat this.

Bonus fact: *It's also said that redheads are the greatest firewalkers on the planet. They are somehow more adept than the average person at navigating the hot coals while avoiding the injurious consequences of such an act ...*

WHY ARE REDHEADS SO PALE? AND WHY CAN'T THEY TAN?

Red hair is associated with fair skin because of redheads' specific genetic makeup. The MC1R gene is the melanocortin-1 receptor, which is found on chromosome 16 and causes low concentrations of eumelanin throughout the body. This can result in red hair as well as fair skin – usually both (though not always).

As to why redheads don't tan ... well, fair skin tends not to. Instead, it's prone to sunburn. And because of the natural tanning reaction to the sun's ultraviolet light, as well as the high amounts of pheomelanin in their skin, redheads commonly have freckles – it's all thanks to that darn recessive gene.

This is why you're likely to see redheads hiding from the sun. For the average redhead, a leisurely trip to the beach is the stuff of nightmares, a tactical mission rather than a chance to flaunt summer abs and soak up some rays.

SPF
GINGER
GRADE

ARE REDHEADS MORE PRONE TO SKIN CANCER CAUSED BY SUN DAMAGE?

Yes. According to *The International Journal of Cancer*, natural redheads are 2.5 times more likely to develop skin cancer than those who possess other hair colours.

Melanin aids UV tolerance, so redheads' lower concentration of melanin seriously hampers the body's ability to deal with UV radiation, leading to a higher risk of skin cancer.

IF EXPOSED TO A LOT OF UV RADIATION, WILL A REDHEAD EXPLODE OR IMPLODE?

While some people like to imagine that redheads, when exposed to high levels of UV radiation, will burn up like a vampire exposed to the sun, this seems highly unlikely.

Instead, we think they might simply melt. You know, like the baddies at the end of *Raiders of the Lost Ark* ...

IS IT TRUE THAT PEOPLE WITH RED HAIR ARE AT GREATER RISK OF DEVELOPING PARKINSON'S DISEASE?

Studies have shown that people with red hair do run a higher risk of developing Parkinson's disease, which is determined by genetic factors. In fact, Tourette syndrome and endometriosis have also been found to be over-represented in the ginger community.

While this might seem a troubling reality for gingers, the flip side is this: given advancements in modern medicine and scientific research, a greater understanding of the genetic preconditions that bring about such medical issues could also help determine treatments and possibly even cures. In redheads, scientists and medical professionals might just find a way to combat some of the modern health threats faced by people today.

IS IT TRUE THAT REDHEADS WITH BLUE EYES ARE A SUPER RACE?

Yes! And the author of this book is in no way biased ... *ahem* ...

But it is true! Well, okay, maybe not the super race thing, but it is true that blue eyes and red hair form the rarest genetic and aesthetic combination in the world. Most natural redheads tend towards shades of brown where eye colour is concerned, with hazel and green eyes close behind in prevalence.

IS IT TRUE THAT GINGERS ONLY EAT ORANGE-COLOURED AND GINGER-THEMED FOODS?

Why bust this myth? Yes, of course. Redheads only eat oranges and ginger root and pumpkins and carrots, which is why they can all see so well in the dark, and why they have such a low level of appreciation for the term carrot-top: *because carrot-tops are green!*

Okay, no, not really. Redheads can eat anything and everything they desire. However, it's worth noting that the colour red was perhaps the very first colour that human beings learned to distinguish – it's the colour of blood and fire, after all. Where food is concerned, it's thought that when our species still lived in the trees, red was an important colour to distinguish, too. How else could we tell the difference between ripe and unripe fruit?

IS IT TRUE THAT REDHEADS ARE MORE LIKELY TO BE LEFT-HANDED?

While little scientific research has been done concerning the apparent left-handed tendencies of gingers, what we do know is that recessive traits commonly come in pairs. Given that both redheadedness and left-handedness are recessive traits, they're sometimes seen together in the one person. It's still not known whether redheads are more commonly left-handed, but it is certainly plausible ...

MARK TWAIN SAID THAT WHILE MOST PEOPLE ARE DESCENDED FROM MONKEYS, REDHEADS ARE DESCENDED FROM CATS. IS THIS TRUE? ARE REDHEADS ACTUALLY CAT-PEOPLE?

Have you ever looked into the eyes of a tabby cat? No? Look into the eyes of a ginger kitty before you next look into the eyes of a ginger. You'll be surprised by what you find ...

Okay, so if that ridiculous method doesn't convince you, at least know this: scientists have reported that Neanderthals also had a version of the gene that causes gingerness, though not the same type that contemporary redheads have.

So, you know, it's either cats or Neanderthals ...

WHY ARE REDHEADS IRRESISTIBLE?

Because red is irresistible! If you're a redhead aficionado, rest assured you're not the only one. Unfortunately for gingers, bees and wasps tend to gravitate towards them, too ...

But who doesn't love a redhead? Red is the colour of fire and passion and blood, representing sex and danger and life itself. It speaks to something primal in the human condition. In the East, red also denotes good fortune. And red is the first colour that comes back to sufferers of brain damage, well before any others. So, it seems we're simply hard-wired for it.

In real terms, their scent and pheromone output, their intelligence and good looks, and their innate ability to produce Vitamin D all make gingers attractive to the world. It's even believed that the reason redheaded women are so sought after by men – the origins of their flame-haired temptress persona – actually stems from a primal understanding that, at least for cavemen, choosing a redhead as a mate would translate into a better chance to breed successfully. But beyond the scientific and the biological, redheads are just really great. Come on, it's obvious. Gingers are awesome!

PLAYBOY MAGAZINE ONCE STATED THAT 'REDHEADS ARE LIKE OTHER WOMEN – ONLY MORE SO.' IS THIS TRUE?

Naturally ... Both in real life and in legend, redheaded women lead incredible lives. Lilith, the first wife of Adam, was ultimately booted from the Garden of Eden. Why? Because she refused to subordinate herself to a man. In the 19th century, criminologist Cesare Lombroso and journalist Guglielmo Ferrero found that red hair was associated with crimes of lust. They concluded that 48 per cent of female criminals were redheads. And on screen, red hair in women has been commonly associated with passion, lust and heightened sexuality – think Rita Hayworth's ultimate femme fatale, Gilda, or the titular protagonist of the 1932 romantic comedy *Red-Headed Woman*, played by Jean Harlow, who is prone to violent temper tantrums and is characterised as a sexually aggressive homewrecker.

RED HAIR IN WOMEN HAS BEEN COMMONLY ASSOCIATED WITH PASSION, LUST AND HEIGHTENED SEXUALITY

Much like the idea that redheads have fiery tempers, the idea that redheaded women are all wild sirens is largely culturally created. However, according to Dr Werner Habermehl, a Hamburg-based sex researcher, women with red hair purportedly have more sex than women of any other hair colour. By extension, Dr Habermehl postulated that non-redheaded women who are in a relationship and who dye their hair red might be signalling that they are unhappy and on the lookout for something else ...

ARE GINGERS MORE PRONE TO WRINKLES?

Unfortunately, yes. However, this isn't something that is necessarily fated. The cause of wrinkles for gingers is the same thing that makes them prone to sunburn and skin cancer – their fair skin. And, of course, sun damage is a cause of wrinkles, too.

So, if you're a ginger, keeping out of the sun remains a priority for many reasons. Proactive redheads, who always carry a cap and sunscreen and remain vigilant about sun protection, should hold up well into old age and avoid their inclination to wrinkle.

ARE REDHEADS SMART?

According to one study, gingers are thought to be four times more likely to become CEOs within a company than their non-redheaded counterparts. But is their intelligence the key factor here? And can we accurately say that redheads generally have higher IQs than the average person?

Well, not really ... Like most research conducted on redheadedness, the data in this study was taken from a small sample size, and the conclusion drawn includes a lot of variables. It is commonly believed that redheads are smart, but this belief, like so many others, might be more culturally generated than scientifically viable.

While gingers cop all sorts of negative generalisations, they benefit from some positive ones, too. Assumptions about their warrior spirit have instilled the idea of redheads being assertive and confident, and with these traits comes competence. It seems likely that it's these perceptions of the redheaded personality that fuel the understanding of their intelligence, something that is advantageous to them in the workplace. So, are they more likely to take on high-powered roles? Yes, probably. But is this because they're smarter? Not necessarily.

> **Bonus fact:** *The notion that gingers are more clever than the average person hasn't always been a good thing. Centuries ago redheads were even believed to have magical powers, and were suspected of being witches …*

DO REDHEADS NATURALLY GENERATE MORE VITAMIN D THAN OTHERS?

Yes. One of the advantages of having paler skin is that it's more efficient at soaking up sunlight, which is of course a requirement for the body to manufacture Vitamin D. So, for those redheads who live in countries with low light conditions (think western Europe, where the weather conditions are cloudier and more prone to rain), their ability to generate Vitamin D, thanks to their lower melanin-concentration, results in a super-boosted immune system that's more adept at fighting off health threats, such as smallpox, plague or consumption.

This can be traced back thousands of years. After humans moved out of Africa and skin tone began to lighten, they began to develop different hair colours, too. As humans moved to parts of the world where there was less sunshine, our bodies developed all kinds of fascinating ways to survive, evolve and thrive. This is just one of them.

> **Bonus fact:** *Remember what we told you about red hair helping cavemen find a mate, potentially giving them a better chance to breed successfully? Well, this is because, for women, the ability to produce Vitamin D could mean they have a stronger pelvis, better able to withstand the trauma of childbirth, as well as a body that could hold up to the rigours of breastfeeding.*

3.

A GINGER STATE OF MIND

While redheads might be few in number, this slim 2 per cent of the global population have had a disproportionate influence on history, shaping both stories and folklore, and even science and culture as we know it today. Perhaps, as pagans once thought, redheads have an aura of magnetism about them, as well as mystical powers, which is why they have had such an impact on the world. Or maybe it's simply because they stand out. But whatever you choose to believe, the information presented in the following chapter makes one thing undeniably clear: gingers have made a difference.

From what they have done, to what has been done to them and, most importantly, who exactly they were, redheads have made a profound impact on the world. History is simply littered with them. Read on to discover the many ways gingers have shaped the world ...

SPECULATIONS OR TRUTH?

ADAM WAS A REDHEAD

It has been speculated that Adam, of Adam and Eve fame, was a natural ginger. This is because the Hebrew word for 'red' is 'adom', as well as the fact that Adam was from 'red earth'. This is perhaps somewhat of a stretch, maybe the work of those keen to read red into all things. Then again, it wouldn't be the first time someone's follicle hue has been adapted to match their legendary status.

REDHEADED SLAVES WERE THE MOST EXPENSIVE OF ALL

According to some historical records, slaves with red hair sometimes cost more than their brunette or blonde counterparts. We're not really sure how good this news is, but it's ... kind of flattering?

THE PREVALENCE OF RED HAIR IN THE BRITISH ISLES HAS INFLUENCED MODERN FAMILY NAMES

Some surnames in both the UK and Ireland demonstrate just how common carrot-tops are to the region. Family names such as Reid (which translates as 'red-haired'), Flynn (deriving from the word 'flann' and meaning 'bright red', 'reddish' or 'ruddy') and Flanary (meaning 'red eyebrow' and deriving from both 'flann' meaning 'red' and 'abhar' meaning 'eyebrow') go a long way to establishing a thriving culture of gingerness north of the equator.

RUSSIA IS NAMED AFTER REDHEADS

Russia means 'land of the reds', but whether this is in honour of redheads or simply the colour red is up for debate. It seems likely that 'Russia' is derived from the name of the founder of the first Russian state, Rurik, a Varangian chieftain of the Rus', more commonly known as a Viking. Some portray Rurik as having red hair, although there isn't enough evidence to support this as hard fact. Nonetheless, Russia and its ancestral history has an inescapable association with the gingers.

ATLANTIS PLAYED A HAND IN CREATING THE FIRST REDHEAD

According to legend – and one of the most speculative legends in ginger mythology – there once was a man, Prince Idon, who, after fleeing his homeland, discovered Atlantis. The story of Prince Idon is also the story of where and how red hair originated. After setting his eyes upon Atlantis and being so blown away by its sunset, Prince Idon fell in love with the dazzling red sky and clouds refracting the sun's rays, and the tree leaves dancing in the wind. The mythical site was imprinted onto the prince, and his wish to capture the beauty of Atlantis resulted in his transformation. His hair turned red like the sky and his face was spotted with freckles as a reminder of those dazzling, dancing leaves.

Accordingly, whenever a person gazes upon the locks of a redhead they, too, see the first sunset of Atlantis; and equally, every ginger is a descendent of Prince Idon, meaning that every carrot-top the world over is a prince or princess of Atlantis.

PERSECUTION

MEDIEVAL ANTI-SEMITISM SAW GINGERS IN THE CROSSHAIRS

Throughout the Middle Ages, red hair became synonymous with the religious heresy of Jews and their rejection of Jesus. In Spanish and Italian works of art, for instance, Judas Iscariot was commonly portrayed as a redhead. Having red hair would remain a trait of villainous characters such as Fagin in Charles Dickens' novel *Oliver Twist*, and Shylock in William Shakespeare's play *The Merchant of Venice*.

Unfortunately, the association wasn't limited to artistic renderings. During the Spanish Inquisition, redheads were identified as being Jewish and therefore persecuted. This wasn't the only time gingers were targeted as a result of their looks …

REDHEADS WERE NEEDED TO COMPLETE POTIONS AND POISONS

In a time when being an alchemist was a real job, not a position held by a character in a fantasy novel, redheads were considered important to the making of spells, potions and poisons. For some spells to work, it was thought that the fat of a flame-haired man was needed. In the Jacobean stage play *Bussy D'Ambois*, written by George Chapman in the early 1600s, the perfect poison is described as including the fat of a redheaded male. And in the 1100s it was said that in order to create gold from copper, a mixture of the blood of a redheaded man and the ashes of a basilisk were needed. Which makes complete sense, given how common basilisks were back in the day …

ANCIENT EGYPTIANS SACRIFICED REDHEADS TO THEIR GODS

Redheads got a pretty raw deal in Ancient Egypt, where making human sacrifices was a common practice. Ginger virgins, mostly women, were considered excellent sacrificial fuel, and were burned alive to appease the gods. But for the god Osiris, male redheads were buried alive. You know, for variety ...

THE REDHEAD MURDERS ...

In modern times, while redheads are no longer sacrificed to the gods, they have still been targeted for savage persecution. In the United States, redheads were the victims of a series of unsolved murders from the iate 1970s until the early 1990s, thought to be the work of an operative serial killer.

In total, it is believed that between six and 11 redheads were murdered across the states of Pennsylvania, Mississippi, Kentucky, Arkansas and Tennessee between 1978 and 1992. The killer is thought to have been a truck driver travelling across these regions.

EVEN WACKIER BELIEFS ABOUT REDHEADS

REDHEADS ARE SYNONYMOUS WITH OCCULTIST SUPERSTITIONS

In simpler times, traits common to the fair-skinned ginger, such as freckles and even moles, were perceived as 'marks of the devil'. These were subsequently considered signs of occultist connections, such as an allegiance to Satan (see page 84 for more information about Lucifer). After all, red hair was generally thought to be a sign of grotesque moral degradation and sexual desire.

The ramifications for such beliefs were seen in witch hunts, where redheads were once again singled out for their follicular flare. Many were burned at the stake after being identified in such a way, with prevalent folklore purporting that they had stolen the fires of hell.

REDHEADS TURN INTO VAMPIRES AFTER THEY DIE. AND SOME OF THEM MIGHT BE WEREWOLVES, TOO …

One pervasive rumour in the world of ginger mythology is that Ancient Greeks believed redheads turned into vampires after they died. But the Ancient Greeks mostly celebrated red hair, which appeared on the heads of glorious statues and on some of their more revered figures, such as Achilles and Aphrodite.

Ginger mythology is plagued by contradictions. But the link between redheads and vampirism is more easily traced to a German treatise on witchcraft first published in 1487: the *Malleus Maleficarum* (*Hammer of Witches*). The book, which had a great impact on the culture of the time, was the second bestseller (after the Bible) for nearly 200 years.

Among its strong endorsement for the need to exterminate witches, the *Malleus Maleficarum* also identified those with red hair and green eyes as being possible werewolves and vampires.

HITLER BANNED MARRIAGE BETWEEN REDHEADS FOR FEAR OF DEVIANT OFFSPRING

This one continues in the tradition of ludicrous beliefs. It seems only fitting that a tyrannical madman such as Adolf Hitler would weigh in here eventually – and it should be noted that his beliefs were held a great deal later than the Middle Ages.

Then again, this one might just be a rumour. Still, it's little wonder such a rumour persists. After all, Hitler had a pretty long list of undesirables, and given that a culture of redhead discrimination existed throughout German history (the *Malleus Maleficarum* was actually penned by a German clergyman, Heinrich Kramer, who wrote the publication under his Latinised name, Henricus Institor), it's easy to see how this rumour has taken root, especially if we consider the connections between redheadedness and medieval anti-Semitism.

REDHEADS ARE BORN OF UNCLEAN SEX

Being that it's also the colour of blood, during the Middle Ages it was thought that a child with red hair had been conceived out of 'unclean sex', the prudish term for copulation during menstruation. It's arguably a logical thought ... if you were a humble farmer in the 1200s, that is.

REDHEADS HAVE NO SOULS ...

There's little to expand upon here. After all, it's just a fact, isn't it?

This inane and common suggestion has become a popular running joke thanks to the help of animated comedy television series *South Park*, which has propagated this myth during several episodes. We can find connections to this notion in the former points that posit gingers are in cahoots with Satan ...

LUCKY CHARMS ...
OR NOT

REDHEADS BRING THE WORST LUCK

According to a British tradition, applicable only on New Year's Day, one's 'first caller' (a house guest or unannounced visitor) will bring about a certain kind of luck ... depending on who they are. It is thought that brunettes bring the best luck, while blondes bring none. Widowers, on the other hand, bring bad luck, which seems kind of harsh. But gingers bring the worst luck of all.

REDHEADS ARE GOOD LUCK!

Conversely, in Poland, redhead sightings are thought to be good luck. Depending on how many gingers you see, well, things just get better and better. Apparently, if you pass three gingers in a row you're guaranteed to win the lottery!

NO, WAIT, REDHEADS ARE ACTUALLY BAD LUCK

In Corsica, a small island in the Mediterranean Sea, redheads are thought to be seriously bad luck. But don't stress too much – there's a cure. If you happen to spot a ginger while in Corsica, do yourself a simple favour: spit (it's okay, you've seen a hideous ginger and need to get the rancid taste out of your mouth) and then turn around in a circle. There. Easy. What a perfectly logical solution to witnessing a fellow human being ...

OH, WAIT, WE'RE WRONG AGAIN. PHEW. GINGERS ARE BACK TO BEING GOOD LUCK!

Don't worry, the Danes have got it covered. In Denmark it is considered a significant honour to bear a child with red hair. So, there you go – good luck, after all.

REDHEADS
THROUGH THE AGES

As we've established, redheads have had their fair share of influence throughout history, helping shape both the world and its culture as we know it today. Here is a list of 20 prominent and important ginger figures for you to familiarise yourself with.

THE FEARSOME FEMME:
BOUDICA

After being flogged and witnessing her daughters raped at the hands of the occupying forces of the Roman Empire, Boudica, a queen of the British Celtic Iceni tribe, went on to lead a bloody uprising against the might of Rome. In her own words, *'It is not as a woman descended from noble ancestry, but as one of the people that I am avenging lost freedom, my scourged body, the outraged chastity of my daughters … This is a woman's resolve; as for men, they may live and be slaves.'*

Sometime in the years 60–61 AD, Boudica and her people killed over 70,000 Romans as she rained terror upon three occupied cities in her native land. While ultimately unsuccessful in removing the Roman Empire from her homeland, Boudica's uprising and death remained a symbol of strength and resolve for centuries to come.

Years later, Boudica's tale was rediscovered and she became famous in the Victorian era. This had a lot to do with her name, which translates into the words 'victory' and/or 'victorious', making its most comparable name 'Victoria'. Thus, it was Queen Victoria herself who came to be seen as Boudica's namesake, and the tale of Boudica was revived, making her a cultural icon of the time. She has lived on as such ever since. Today, a statue, Boadicea and Her Daughters, sculpted from bronze by English artist Thomas Thornycroft, stands in central London. The statue depicts Boudica in her war chariot accompanied by her two daughters. The chariot is led by two rearing horses as Boudica stands in a pose of defiance – a spear in one hand and her other hand raised in the air.

THE GRAND RULER:
ELIZABETH I

Good Queen Bess was the daughter of Henry VIII and Anne Boleyn, which is a pretty remarkable duo to have as parents. But more importantly, and the reason she's on this list: Queen Elizabeth I was a ginger. Sure, she had something of an interesting life, too – like the time she was accused of conspiracy and imprisoned for almost a year, or the time her mother was beheaded on charges of incest and adultery and plotting to kill the king.

And, okay, Liz might've done some stuff, too, like defeating the Spanish Armada and queening it up for a good 45-year reign – a time we now refer to as the Elizabethan era, a time in which the arts flourished and English drama was revolutionised by the likes of Christopher Marlowe and William Shakespeare, and in which seafaring adventurers, such as Francis Drake, brought pride to England. And she might've become something of a cult-like figure among her people, who honoured Queen Liz in their art and in their celebrations, mesmerised by her idiosyncrasies, such as her purported virginity.

Sure, all of the above is true, but we all know the real reason Queen Elizabeth I was so great was because she had red hair. It was that MC1R gene what done it.

MODERN MONARCH ... ONE DAY:
PRINCE HARRY

Prince Henry of Wales (Prince Harry to most of us) keeps alive the tradition of redheaded royals. And his stint in Australia, where he worked on a cattle station after graduating from Eton in 2003, might have helped keep those follicles freshly flaming courtesy of the outback sun.

While some might remember him for his tabloid scandals (the ginger community does not endorse dressing up like Hitler, by the way), the young prince's party animal days are far behind him. Today he's a pretty darn good representative of gingerdom – he's seen military action, after all; he even knows how to fly a helicopter, for crying out loud. And then there's his humanitarian work: he's an ambassador for both children in need and wounded soldiers.

Watch out folks. This is one ginger who might actually reign supreme.

SIMPLY RED:
MICK HUCKNALL

With a band named Simply Red, charismatic lead singer Mick Hucknall is not only a fellow redhead, he's an ambassador of gingerdom. After Hucknall's first band, The Frantic Elevators, split, he and his manager put together a new group in 1985. The group was to be called 'Red' in honour of Hucknall's flame-coloured hair, and the nickname he'd had for his entire life. Mick decided to add 'Simply' to the beginning, and the rest, as they say, is history. With over 50 million records sold and a slew of pop hits such as 'Fairground' and 'Stars', Simply Red has become an icon of the ginger music landscape.

But Mick hadn't always been a super-success. He grew up in a single-parent household, raised by his barber father, and ran amok as a teen, finding school depressing and boring. Like all gingers, the Huckster has copped his fair share of follicle flack, especially at school. In his own words: 'I'd get hit and punched and there was a kid who used to do these weird drawings of me with red hair. It was just the most bizarre thing. It was all purely because I had bright red hair.'

Today, however, Hucknall is mostly known for two things: 1) Being a heartthrob of the 1980s and a lothario of legendary proportions (he once dated Catherine Zeta-Jones, FYI), and 2) Being one of the greatest blue-eyed soul singers of all time.

Not bad for a ginger.

THE SPICE OF LIFE:
GINGER SPICE

Ginger Spice isn't just some run-of-the-mill pop diva. She was an icon and a member of the most successful female pop group of all time, the Spice Girls, who sold over 85 million records worldwide. The group's first single, 'Wannabe', debuted at number one in 1996, and they soon became a global phenomenon, not only as a music group, but as a marketing juggernaut, developing a brand that included a range of merchandise and even a film, *Spiceworld*. It's been reported that during their active years, the Spice Girls grossed between $500–800 million.

As one-fifth of the iconic group, Ginger Spice, aka Geri Halliwell, helped give meaning to slogans like 'Girl Power' and 'Cool Britannia'. And let's not forget the fashion. The Spice Girls set so many of the trends we associate with female fashion in the 1990s, including double-bun hairdos and Buffalo platform shoes. Perhaps best remembered of their slew of ensembles was Ginger's iconic Union Jack dress, finished off with red boots, which she wore to the 1997 Brit Awards. The dress would go on to set a Guinness World Record when it was sold at a charity auction for over £40,000 – the most expensive item of clothing ever sold by a pop star at the time.

Testament to Ginger's importance in the group and her place in music history is the fact that it was her departure from the Spice Girls that ended their reign as queens of the music biz. Halliwell would go on to have a successful career as a solo artist, albeit as a blonde, in a bid to distinguish her new career from her previous one. And while hits like 'It's Raining Men' and 'Mi Chico Latino' might have helped solidify her legacy in the annals of British music history, it's her appearance as the flame-haired Ginger Spice that she'll always be best remembered for.

HEROINE CHIC:
AGENT SCULLY

One half of the super-agent duo Fox Mulder and Dana Scully, the lead protagonists of pop culture phenomenon *The X-Files*, FBI Agent Scully is one of the most celebrated female characters in TV history. For her portrayal of Agent Scully across the sci-fi show's many seasons, actress Gillian Anderson received an Emmy Award, a Golden Globe, two SAG Awards and a Saturn Award, though these wins do little justice to the 25 nominations she had for these awards over time.

Dana Scully is both an FBI agent and a medical doctor, and it is her Catholic faith that serves as both a cornerstone and a contrast in her characterisation. Her Catholic beliefs are contrasted with her scepticism of the paranormal elements explored within the show, putting her at odds with her paranormal 'believer' partner, Agent Mulder. But it's in these contrasts and contradictions that viewers of the show found a genuinely strong, likeable and human character with whom they could relate, making her arguably the greatest and most iconic sci-fi heroine ever portrayed. In the words of *X-Files* creator Chris Carter: 'It's Scully's show.'

Agent Scully would go on to influence many female characters on the small screen, including the likes of Veronica Mars, Temperance 'Bones' Brennan and *Elementary*'s Joan Watson, who all embody Scully's blend of resilience and strength. As well as inspiring other female characters on television, Agent Scully has also influenced many women in real life. What is today known as 'The Scully Effect' refers to the observed phenomenon of young women pursuing careers in the fields of science, medicine and law enforcement as a direct result of having been inspired by their favourite ginger heroine: FBI Agent Dana Scully.

FULL-TIME BADASS NINJA:
CHUCK NORRIS

After serving in the Korean War, where he was first exposed to martial arts, Chuck Norris began teaching karate lessons in his backyard before going on to open his first martial arts studio. Soon the Chuckster had a booming business, boasting 30 studios in total, and he became sensei to some of Hollywood's most elite stars, including the likes of Steve McQueen and Priscilla Presley.

It was after his exposure to these Hollywood A-listers that Norris got into the movie biz himself, establishing a successful career co-starring alongside martial arts legend Bruce Lee before finding his stride as lead in a slew of films. Perhaps most notably, Chuck Norris would later portray the protagonist Cordell Walker in the long-running television series *Walker, Texas Ranger*.

While mostly known for his TV and film work, this is one ginger not to be messed with. Norris held the World Middleweight Karate Championship title six times, defending it over consecutive years, and became the first person in the Western Hemisphere to complete an 8th degree Black Belt Grand Master title. He even founded his own form of martial arts, a hybrid fighting style called Chun Kuk Do, which means 'The Universal Way'.

Possessing such legendary macho status, Norris is perhaps best-known today for the series of memes that plague the internet in his honour, and which have helped maintain his mystique as one of the ginger community's most heroic figures. The memes, which fall under the collective title of 'Chuck Norris Facts', detail fictive, ironic and mostly absurd facts pertaining to Chuck's character and his feats of heroism. For instance: did you know that when Chuck Norris does a push-up, he doesn't push himself up? Instead, he pushes the earth down.

THE MANIC ARTIST:
VINCENT VAN GOGH

What's left to say about a man who once cut off a piece of his own ear? Well, apart from the fact that Vinnie Van G was one of the greatest post-impressionist painters in existence, he was also a carrot-top. But then, you probably knew this already. Of all his paintings, Van Gogh's self-portraits are arguably his most iconic and best-known works, as recognisable as the *Mona Lisa* or a postcard of the Eiffel Tower.

This series of self-portraits, painted between 1885 and 1889, puts the Dutchman's ginger beard prominently on display, often contrasted against bold blue tones, each of his much-admired brushstrokes rendering the flaming follicles that shelter his chin and cheeks. You can clearly see the mental demons Van Gogh was wrestling with in his steely eyes. Sadly, he would die by his own hand at the age of 37.

Regardless of the tragic circumstances of his life and death, Van Gogh will go (*gogh?*) down in history as one of the most celebrated and influential artists of all time. In an all-too-short career, he managed to produce over 2000 paintings, most of them landscapes, portraits, self-portraits and still lifes. Not only a famous artist, Van Gogh was quite possibly the most famous redhead the world will ever know.

THE LAUGH MASTER:
LOUIS C.K.

Red-haired comedian Louis C.K. is arguably the funniest man on the planet alive today (depending on your sense of humour, of course). And while he might be balding a little on top, his beard and moustache make up for that missing patch – and the facial hair is as glorious and as ginger as ever, too.

Born in 1967, C.K. began his comedic career writing for famed comedians such as Chris Rock, Conan O'Brien and David Letterman before starring in the short-lived and mostly forgotten sitcom *Lucky Louie*. It took a while for C.K. to find his groove, but it's through his partially autobiographical (and sometimes surreal) television show, *Louie*, that his star has risen. The show blends what has become his trademark dark, vulgar and self-deprecating humour with insightful observations on the human condition and heartfelt renderings of the struggles of parenthood and ageing in contemporary society.

With six Emmy Awards under his belt, and having recently been ranked fourth in *Rolling Stone*'s list of the 50 greatest comedians of all time, checking out this flame-haired laugh master's side-splitting stand-up sets is a must.

LORD OF DARKNESS:
LUCIFER

Lucifer, Satan, the Devil, Lord of Darkness, the Baddest Dude Under the Planet. So many titles for just one man. Or, one hoofed creature with horns and that ... tail thing. And sometimes he has a split tongue, too, right? Is he even a *he*? Actually, now that we think about it ...

Okay, so clearly portrayals of the devil are open to interpretation, but if there's one thing they generally have in common, it's that he/she/it is **RED**. You don't need to be religious to have heard of the devil, and you'd have to be living under a rock not to have seen some rendering of Lucifer by now. But why red?

Well, as we've discussed, red is associated with quite a lot of things. It is the colour of fire and blood, imagery suited to the depths of Hell, where the devil resides. Red has also traditionally been viewed as the colour of sexual desire and moral degradation, which is the reason a lot of redheads have been persecuted in connection with occultist practices – witch burning and the like. So, yeah, Satan, the Devil, whatever you want to call him and whatever form he takes, is red, and this kind of makes him something of an uber-ginger.

Is the ginger community proud to call the Lord of Darkness one of their own? Are they in fact evil devil worshippers, as witch hunters once suspected? Who the hell knows!

PURE GENIUS: GALILEO GALILEI

Even if he's not the most recognisable ginger, and not even the most famous redhead to date, Galileo might just be the ginger community's most celebrated and greatest mind. After all, you don't wind up being called the 'father of science' for nothing. In fact, Galileo's been called the 'father of modern physics' *and* the 'father of scientific method' *and* the 'father of observational astronomy', too! He obviously did something right ...

Born in 1564, Galileo Galilei was an Italian polymath who made contributions in various scientific fields, including astronomy, engineering, physics and mathematics. Most notably, Galileo's work and theories contributed significantly to the scientific revolution of his era. However, it was this work and theory that also contributed to his alienation within a century governed by Holy Scripture.

From 1610–1633 a sequence of events known as 'the Galileo affair' transpired, in which Galileo's scientific theories and findings were investigated by a Roman Inquisition because the Catholic Church found them heretical. Ultimately, Galileo was found suspect of heresy in 1633 and sentenced to indefinite imprisonment. He remained under house arrest until he passed away in 1642. He left behind a monumental scientific legacy that included the discovery of the four largest satellites of the planet Jupiter, known today as the Galilean moons.

CRAZED AND CONFUSED:
LYNETTE 'SQUEAKY' FROMME

Maybe not the best representative for the redhead community, but a ginger nonetheless, Lynette Fromme found herself a part of the Manson Family – a notorious commune-cum-cult of lost souls led by murderous psychopath Charles Manson – in 1967, having dropped out of college and become homeless following an argument with her father.

She would go on to live with the Mansons in the desert near Death Valley, and in Southern California at their compound on Spahn Ranch, where George Spahn gave her the nickname 'Squeaky'. Why 'Squeaky' you ask? Well, because of the noise she made whenever old George touched her ... hmmmm.

While Squeaky was not involved in the infamous Manson Family murders that occurred in 1969, in which pregnant actress Sharon Tate lost her life, Fromme remained a staunch supporter of Charles Manson and his cause, keeping a vigil outside the courthouse during the Mansons' trial. Her vigil did little to lessen the impact of the life sentences that were handed down, however, and it would be several more years before Lynette became known as anything other than a Manson loyalist.

On 5 September, 1975, Fromme went to see US President Gerald Ford at a public appearance in Sacramento's Capitol Park. She was there to raise the President's awareness about the plight of the local environment, and took a pistol with her to make her point. But despite there being no bullet in the chamber of the gun (though the magazine was loaded), it turned out that waving a gun at a US President is kind of a big deal, and Squeaky was arrested and thrown in jail to serve a life sentence. In an interview given in 1987, Fromme stated that she didn't regret what she had done, and that 'it was fate'. However, she did state that her lengthy incarceration was a bit 'unnecessary', given that she never even fired her pistol.

In August 2009 after serving 34 years behind bars, Lynette 'Squeaky' Fromme was finally released from prison. At the age of 60 her hair wasn't as joyfully ginger as it was in 1975, but hey, a redhead nonetheless.

CLASSIC BEAUTY:
RITA HAYWORTH

First things first: Rita Hayworth was NOT a natural redhead. But her impact as a dye-job was important enough that she still sneaks onto this list. After all, it was her portrayal of the titular femme fatale in the 1946 film noir *Gilda* that perhaps contributed the most to ginger mythology in the past century, particularly where redheads' lusty, sensual qualities are concerned. While some may argue that this is a bad thing, it is worth noting that the mythos surrounding redheads is unusually gendered. This seems to be one of the rare times that, when it comes to stereotypes, women actually get the better deal.

Since the Classical world, redheaded males have been seen mostly as barbarians – the Greeks thought so, and even Alexander the Great made an effort to recruit them into his armies – while today red hair in men is commonly thought of as nerdy and wimpish. And while we don't want to celebrate a sexualised portrayal of the female form, being perceived as a siren of great beauty and wonder certainly trumps caveman or uber-dork. This is where Rita Hayworth steps in.

Hayworth was one of the biggest stars in Hollywood during the 1940s. She was a pin-up girl and icon to American GIs during World War II – gorgeous, yes, coveted, most definitely, but also a reminder of home and of the bountiful wonder and beauty that awaited their return. She was a reason to fight, a reprieve from a cold trench and a symbol of the causes being fought for – hope, freedom and the Western world. For all these reasons, we can forgive the hair dye. She may not have been a natural, but this redhead is one the ginger community feels comfortable embracing.

NOT IN KANSAS ANYMORE:
JUDY GARLAND

In her lifetime, friend o' gingers and the LGBTQI community Judy Garland won a Golden Globe Award, a Cecil B. DeMille Award, a Tony Award, two Grammys, a Grammy Lifetime Achievement Award, was inducted into the Grammy Hall of Fame, and was nominated for an Emmy Award three times and an Academy Award twice. (She also snatched up an Academy Juvenile Award as a youngster, but they don't really hand those out anymore, so ...)

Garland worked as an actress for years under a studio contract with MGM, commonly starring alongside funny man Mickey Rooney. But when her contract expired, Judy took her career to the stage, playing concerts to packed-out theatres across America and becoming a music legend, famed for her contralto voice, beloved by the gay community and celebrated by gingers everywhere.

Best known for her role as Dorothy in 1939's musical film *The Wizard of Oz*, the image of Garland in her iconic blue and white dress, her gorgeous red plaits framing her porcelain face, her doll-like eyes at once inquisitive, pleading and innocent, is pop culture iconography at its most pure.

ORPHANED BUT NOT FORGOTTEN: ANNE OF GREEN GABLES & LITTLE ORPHAN ANNIE

Okay, so we're killing two birds with one stone here, but both are worth mentioning, and they pair somewhat nicely in a single entry. These two young, female flame-haired characters from the early 20th century share more than just the MC1R gene: they're both orphans, of course. Oh, and their names are practically identical.

It's worth reflecting upon why these two little orphaned girls were both portrayed as redheads. The answer here seems threefold: red hair connotes a level of alienation befitting a child who has no biological parents; red hair conveys a strength of will, representing that much talked about 'fieriness' (Annie is something of an adventurer, while it is said of Anne that 'her temper matches her hair'); and, finally, red hair is used sympathetically, much in the same way that it is often employed in modern advertisements, being at once cutesy and playful, fun and innocent, and a little bit naughty, too.

Anne of Green Gables was a children's novel published in 1908 that follows the life of titular heroine, 11-year-old Anne, who is accidentally sent to live with a middle-aged brother and sister on a farm. The novel has sold over 50 million copies in 20 different languages. *Little Orphan Annie*, on the other hand, started life as a daily comic strip in the United States and followed the adventures of Annie and her dog Sandy. Since then, the comic strip has been adapted into a series of successful musicals for stage and screen – who hasn't heard of the musical *Annie*?

Both girls started out life innocently enough, but with their spunk and pizzazz, both became international sensations and ambassadors of gingerdom. And we're equally proud of them both!

THE SOULFUL POET:
SYLVIA PLATH

Out of the ash
I rise with my red hair
And eat men like air.

These immortal lines are taken from Sylvia Plath's poem 'Lady Lazarus', which was originally published posthumously in 1965 in the collection *Ariel*. The poem uses German imagery while also dealing with themes of death, failure and resurrection. 'Lady Lazarus' describes the speaker's unsuccessful suicide attempts, finally ending in her rebirth as a mythical bird, the phoenix, which in mythology rose from the ashes. Critics are divided as to the message these final lines convey – a demonic transformation or a change in direction?

Plath is best remembered as a poet and for the tragic way she ended her life, committing suicide at the age of 30 after years of depression. However, there's far more to Plath than a handful of poems and an early death. She was, and continues to be, one of the great shapers of cultural, literary and feminist intellectualism in the modern era, her voice speaking to the generations of women, writers, academics and cultural theorists that have followed. And nor was she solely a poet. Her novel, *The Bell Jar*, remains one of the seminal works of roman à clef narrative prose (a form of fictionalised autobiography). The book, which details the struggles of growing up, has been popular among young readers since its publication in 1963.

WORLD LEADER:
WINSTON CHURCHILL

There are few people you'd want more in your corner during a crisis than Winston Churchill. The former British Prime Minister's legacy was solidified during the war-ridden decades of the early 20th century, a time during which Mr Churchill is believed to have played a hand in defending the United Kingdom from the terror of the Nazi regime and Adolf Hitler's world-dominating political strategy. And it just so happens that Churchill was a redhead to boot.

Churchill's shadow as Prime Minister looms large over the course of modern history, but it shouldn't be forgotten that before he took office in Parliament, he was already an immensely successful man, and quite a well-known British figure. He was a writer – both a journalist and an author – who penned several works of non-fiction. He also published a novel and a short story, and in 1953 he received the Nobel Prize in Literature. Both his written work and his work as an orator (he wrote his own speeches, too!) made Churchill an important historian and human rights activist, his Nobel Prize win distinguishing him for his historical and biographical depictions and for his defence of human values.

It's also worth remembering that Churchill was a soldier before World War I, and was re-elected as Prime Minister for a second time after World War II, in 1951. While he will most commonly be remembered for his actions during the years 1939–1945, his achievements and successes were far more expansive. He will go down in history not only as a great politician, but one of the greatest men and one of the greatest leaders the free world has ever seen. Ginger pride, indeed!

HAPPY DAYS:
RON HOWARD

Listing actor and director Ron Howard's credits is an exercise in patience – the list goes on and on and on and ... The point is, he's a legend of the screen, both small and silver, who became known through starring roles in sitcoms, most notably as the protagonist of long-running series *Happy Days*, in which he played Ritchie Cunningham. People might remember the show thanks to Henry Winkler's iconic character 'The Fonz', but Howard's Cunningham was a big reason the show lasted into an eleventh season, right up to that moment they literally and officially 'jumped the shark' (an act that has since become a figurative statement in common parlance).

It's always nice to see a ginger in the limelight, and helming a beloved TV franchise is certainly an honour, but Howard's career and powers of gingerness go far beyond appearances in a now-dated sitcom. No, like all good carrot-tops, Howard won't be finished amazing the world until he's dead and buried, which is why he now directs movies. He directed *Apollo 13* and *Frost/Nixon*, and won an Oscar for *A Beautiful Mind*, and convinced Tom Hanks to make a spectacle of himself solving the greatest puzzle of the modern age, *The Da Vinci Code* ... (It's not a movie, it's a documentary. You heard it here first ...)

Oh yeah, and Ron Howard has not one, but two – *two* – stars on the Hollywood Walk of Fame. That's right, it's impressive. But then, that's just what gingers do.

THE STUFF OF NIGHTMARES: BRAM STOKER

As far as shaping the collective consciousness of the modern world is concerned, Bram Stoker rates pretty highly. Bram Stoker is of course the 19th century Irish author best known as the creator of Count Dracula, who first appeared in Stoker's 1897 novel *Dracula.* Within the book, Stoker established so many of the conventions and characteristics we associate with vampire mythology and lore today. Since its publication, the inspired works of art, literature and screen adaptations that the novel has spawned have been innumerable, and the legacy of the ongoing feud between Stoker's characters has lived on in the collective imagination of generations since.

The battle between Count Dracula and the novel's protagonist, Professor Abraham Van Helsing, is an age-old fight between good and evil and light and darkness, and we can only imagine it will continue to entertain, terrify and enchant those who encounter its renderings for centuries more to come.

At this point, do we really need to mention the colour of Mr Stoker's hair?

Way to shape the world, gingers!

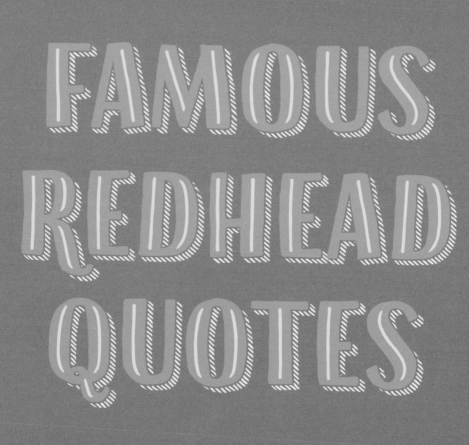

FAMOUS
REDHEAD
QUOTES

'RED HAIR IS GREAT. IT'S RARE, AND THEREFORE SUPERIOR.'

– Augusten Burroughs

'PEOPLE WITH RED HAIR ARE SUPPOSED TO GET MAD VERY EASILY, BUT ALLIE NEVER DID, AND HE HAD VERY RED HAIR.'

– Holden Caulfield

'MAN, YOU AIN'T LIVED 'TIL YOU'VE HAD YOUR TIRES ROTATED BY A REDHEADED WOMAN.'

– Bruce Springsteen

'RED HAIR, SIR, IN MY OPINION, IS DANGEROUS.'

– P.G. Wodehouse

'WHEN RED-HEADED PEOPLE ARE ABOVE A CERTAIN SOCIAL GRADE THEIR HAIR IS AUBURN.'

– Mark Twain